# FAR FROM BROKEN

Also by Kelsey Bigelow

*Sprig of Lilac*
*Depression Holders and Secret Keepers*
*The Coffee Cherry*

# Far From Broken

## A Poetry Collection

Kelsey Bigelow

Cover photo by Janet Eckles.

Published in the United States by Kindle Direct Publishing.

First edition, 2024.

kelkaybpoetry.com

ISBN: 979-8-8691-5850-5
Imprint: Indy Pub

*For those who need someone who will listen*

*"You have already been faced with some challenges that many people will never face. You come from what society calls a 'broken family,' yet you are far from broken."*

*— Dad (2008)*

## Contents

# INTRODUCTION

# DEAR READER,

I hope you do not relate to what's ahead. If you do, I hope you see that you are not alone, and a better life is possible. We all go through messy, heavy stuff throughout our lives. What's most important is how we allow ourselves to cope, process, and heal.

If you do relate, please know you are braver than you may give yourself credit for. In 2008, I wrote the following in my notebook:

> *They say, "You're so brave for going through every day happy." But I'm not that strong. I cry almost every day. I break down at least once a week. I can't handle all the stuff going on.*

In 2023, I realized I was braver than I ever knew. As I entered my 30s and exited my dissociation, I realized I was in the same place I was 15 years before. I cried almost every day. I had panic attacks at least once a week. I often felt like I couldn't handle everything that was happening. Except this time, I could recognize that I'm strong enough to keep going and not separate myself from it all.

I've learned that bravery means doing it scared and uncertain. Bravery is learning to hold the heavy alongside the hopeful and joyful. Bravery is choosing to stay present and feel all the feelings as they come. Bravery is not having the answers or knowing when the load will lighten but choosing to keep going.

Bravery is holding your 15-year-old-self's hand and telling them, "We can do this together. One day at a time."

Please note: Multiple things can be true at once. This collection is as I experienced my life. There is a lot of grief, pain, and traumas discussed in these pages. However, my experiences do not negate the fact that the people in these stories were doing the best they could with what they had.

There has been significant healing and growth by me and others. The past may have been painful with lingering effects, but the present is beautiful as we heal together.

ALL THE BEST,
KELSEY BIGELOW

## Dear Young Lost Writer,

I hear you asking for mile markers and a rerouting to get you to where I am. I need you to know you'll get there. I need you to know it won't be easy. I know life feels like unending concrete right now. I hear it in your questions. You're in a sea of no-one-prepared-me.

I know joy was smacked out of your backbone, but it's time to bring it back yourself. You have all the tools to build away from the familiar and to craft your own happiness despite their harm. It's okay to do exactly what your gut knows is best.

I hear you seeking validation and the right answers, but only you know those.

If I could tell you anything to help you get through, I'd tell you it gets better if you make it better. You can make your life what you want it to be. You can choose who you have in your life and who knows details about you. You don't have to let everyone access every part of your life.

You can make decisions on your own and not tell the people who will alter your choices until it's too late for them to impact it. You can change your mind. You're never too far into something or someone to learn it's not right for you and to change course.

You don't have to stay in one place simply because it's familiar. Meeting new streets and faces goes a long way in meeting yourself.

Take the leaps you can't stop thinking about. Most big decisions are not permanent. Doing what you want to do instead of what everyone expects of you makes life so much better.

You may be broken from a life you didn't ask for, but you are far from broken. You can build and heal into the life you dream of. The life you're meant for. I'm living proof of that.

Your answer won't be poetic or in a form you know. It'll be a messy free verse that you draft and edit and rearrange over and over. Never ending. But it'll be yours. It'll reflect you, not them. You have the power to do so.

You may feel like you don't know the path. But your gut and heart? They know. Trust them.

You're allowed to write your own life. I give you permission to leave what hurts you and choose what helps you. This advice applies to every part of life — people, career, hobbies, passions, pastimes, where you live, what you drive, what you eat and wear, how you talk, all of it.

Your skepticism seems to cloud your ability to believe me, and I don't blame you for that. You've had many adults prove themselves untrustworthy and harmful. I hope you see the honesty in me and trust my story to be proof that I'm simply telling you what worked for me.

I can only hope that something I say might help you too. You deserve it.

Take a breath. Take a step. Take your life into your own grasp and live it how you want. I promise that you can.

## MY HONEST POEM
AFTER RUDY FRANCISCO

Hi
My name is Kelsey
I'm 5' 3"
a mediocre yogi
and have met only one person paler than me

All of that rhymed and
it was only 3/4 intentional
I live with dissociation and C-PTSD
so I often hide behind weighted blankets
and free form poetry

I like driving without a destination
and meeting new dogs
though I prefer cats in my home
I think this is because
my childhood was nomadic
with a bark that wouldn't quit

I will share more on the mic
than my family would like
but helping others feel understood
is what brought me to the stage

I love a good Greek salad
but I don't do olives
I barely do the feta

I don't really have any secrets
I'm not sure if that's a good or bad thing yet
and I hope I never find out

I like my coffee black
and my bookshelves full

I'm oddly good at eating Sloppy Joes
without being sloppy

Probably from training myself
to keep my messes hidden

I don’t know a lot
but I know every line to *Gilmore Girls*
and that I have survived 100% of my worst days

I know that poetry is my ultimate metaphor
as I choose which lines to break
which rhymes to make
while I write my life into its own rhythm
Because I was a young girl in Chucks
fighting sandpaper days and turning scrapes into poetry

And I know that all of this
has made me who I am here today

A young woman
building marble years
a poetry career
and still wearing Chucks

MY POEMS NOW
are not a cry for help
My poems now
are because I cried for help years ago
and the only one who listened
was my notebook

# [Written at 18]

Memory often fails me
losing myself in the madness
feeling directionless
reflectionless
But the page holds my place
makes itself anything I may need that day
like a mirror
a compass
a white noise machine
a memory
The page is my lineless welcome mat
bringing me home
so I can see myself in the words

## DIGRESSION

Writing
is the last thing
I want to do

I don’t really know why this is
because writing
is the only thing
I need to do

Maybe it has something to do with the fact that
shedding a layer of my heart
and molding it into words on a page
for all to read means
molding it into words on a page for all to read

Maybe it’s because
I have been actively shaping my self-esteem
into a genuine mirror of a mastered smile and
everyone knows that
a happy poem
is almost always an oxymoron

Maybe it's because
speaking the dissonance of my soul
breaks the innocence I've learned to portray
and ruins the ignorant ears
of those who think they know me
like the ones who ask why
a coffee snob like me hasn’t had any coffee
yet today and it’s already 11 a.m.
I say nothing and instead turn to my notebook
and explain to the page that
I haven’t had coffee
because I haven’t had a full meal in a while
because I haven’t had enough money for such a luxury
and so I drink water to ignore the rumbles
and to say thank you
to the years I struggled with anorexia

because they taught me how to fake my health
they taught me how to get through a day without fainting
in order to get the body I thought I was supposed to want
a body that men would want to touch        not take
but they didn't take
they stole
They stole a body I grew to loathe
but then again I'm told to be grateful for the body that I'm in
because the body that I'm in has so much built-in privilege
that it has become translucent
but the thing about being translucent
is that no one sees me
which means loneliness goes to bed with me
and shapeshifts into the depression that is my body
I digress

This is why I avoid writing
because only after reading my own words
do I begin to sort trauma from struggle
and only after reading my own words
do I realize

I've got too much to write about

## LOOK CLOSER

Insomnia has me up at 1 a.m. thinking about this poem
thinking about all of my poems
How they wrote my way through a neglectful pestilence

If you line them up just right
they make a flipbook of a viscous quest
where I battle my fear of being insignificant

A quest where I fight the dinosaurs I outgrew
along the way to creating my own lustrous life
and planting pinecones in lands they'll never know

If you lay my poems out just right
you can see how each line became the scaffolding
I used to brace myself
against the punchiness of this story

You can see how each stanza helped me slow my tempo
to design an adagio I want to dance along with
Listen closely to my alliterations across all the pages

you may hear an amethyst melody
a cleansing of each lifestyle I've lived
Sometimes they sounded like Boys Like Girls or Weezer

other seasons heard more of Taylor Swift or Ira Wolf
with a smattering of Celtic and Spanish styles mixed in

If you read my poems just right you will see
how the adventures in these rhythms saved my life

## THIS IS A STORY ABOUT A SELF-LOVE JOURNEY

It’s quiet

but in a
“gulp back cry sounds on the shoulder of my pillow so as not to
disturb the disruption”
kind of way

It’s about learning to parent    not finger paint    and
hiding when the footsteps get heavier
It’s hungry

But in a
di s a p p e a r i n g    way

It’s about looking 12 years old    at 16
counting bites    and comparing arm size

This story is about
forcing my reflection
into a mirror occupied
by whoever tried to
love me at the time

It's    subtle
but in a "no one called me out"    kind of way

or a

“dig the key in softly
enough so the arm spots
only light up purple
when I'm cold”
way

It’s about building definitions from the trusted who injected
bitterness into my scale and smile

It's easily unnoticed

but in a
"only tell my notebook
because no one believes my C-PTSD or depression anyway"
kind of way

This story is about deciding
to make a minivan
my home and
begging it to survive
every day

It's about breathing through the lonely
and finding my sewable pieces

It's m es s y
but not in a visible way

More like a "rely on sticky cup holders and coffee-stained
directions to get to my first home" way

or a

"Realize my broken parts didn't die in the shoebox under my old twin bed"

and "unbury my coping mechanisms in the tote my parents sent me"
kind of way

It's messy in a
"clear off cobweb journals
and learn from my past self"
kind of way

This story is about letting
the decades-old graphite wear off
on my thumb
because I finally learned
how to wash it off

# BEHEMOTH

My childhood was a war
Each lost battle finding myself scarred
wilted like a malodorous pumpkin
in the deep hungers of autumn
left to cradle itself
like the afterthought it was

My memories abandoned their home
while swinging sweetly from a branch
as if they were leaves playing
in the light breeze and not
dying of loneliness
trampled by elephants and trust issues

I drag this Behemoth everywhere I go
Its gaze watches me in the plane window
scans into a subway train with me
and lies next to me on my bathroom floor
as I beg it to let me lift myself up
to forge my own abundance without it
to create a home
where this lack of reflection
can shine peacefully

But for now
the weight is too much
and my memories have blown away

All I can do is lie here
holding my Purple Heart

# SILVER LININGS

If you ask how I manage to see the silver linings
among the flecks of smut I'm constantly cleaning
off my back and the mayhem I was burgeoned into
I won't tell you how I avoid it all by lying to you
how I disguise the tartness of my story as rhubarb
and the sour chapters as a limoncello
how I know that the sweet scenes are as rare as lobster

I won't tell you of the years I fought my own solipsism
to become someone worthy of trust
someone you could look to for instruction
You can't see the effort I put in
to become the goddess of invisibility
to control which parts of myself I show you

If you ask how I manage to see the silver linings
because you see someone indissoluble and alpha-like
I will hope that you don't test my strength with a touchstone
because it will reveal everything I've hidden from you

It will reveal the nights I lie awake
wishing I had narcolepsy
so I could stop meeting 2 a.m.
stop imagining being born into a different caste
It will reveal the days I envied the clouds
wishing my god was Zeus and I were a virga
because then all I would have to do
to receive no more punishments
is evaporate and fulfill my purpose

If you ask how I manage to see the silver linings
I will tell you
I simply don't see any other way
to survive

## ALLOW ME TO REINTRODUCE MYSELF

You know
I find it bonkers
that we don't know much about each other
So allow me to reintroduce myself

Hi
My name is abnormal
like born in the southern tip of an Illinois divorce
with brothers born
under the gateway of a St. Louis shadow
and in the white sands a couple hours shy
of Albuquerque and a normal life

But let's not get into that
Let's keep this light

Hi
My name is effervescent
like energizing our conversation with laughs
and sharing in our sarcasm spiritual
but also like facading vivaciousness
feeling the fakeness in the crook of my elbow
perhaps that's why I can't peel them from my sides

But that's veering to the heavy
Let's start over

Hi
My name is pleasant
like warming your arms into a hug
before we even say hi
and being voted most likely
to brighten your day in high school
But also like never causing a scene
because disruption was never my favorite word
I once tried to disguise it as hullabaloo
but commotion couldn't hide between flinches

Sorry
there's the heavy again
I have a habit of oversharing

I just want you to know
my name is also tempest
like I'm used to being knocked off my feet
laced with tragedy and gusted
into my next dissociative state
Always feeling forgotten
not realizing I forgot myself
Though I'm here
and still learning
to accept my hopeless years

Sorry
we got to the heavy again
Let's start over

Hi my name is Kelsey
and I'll share all my veiled parts if you ask
but right now
I'd like to know more about you
What's your name again?

# TONING DOWN

# MEMORY: 4 YEARS OLD

"No, we have to get this done before your dad picks you up. Just don't tell him what we're doing, okay?" Mom says as she holds my 4-year-old hand begging to see Mall Santa.

I follow her because she's on a mission, and I don't want her or Dad to be mad again. She sits me in a tall chair at the purple jewelry store.

"Do you like these pretty little flower ones?" Mom asks me, holding up a piece of colored cardboard with small white flower earrings on it.

I see how happy she looks, so I smile and nod.

"We'll do these ones, thanks." Mom says to the lady with orange spikes in her ears.

The lady tells me, "Okay sweetheart, I'm going to hold this gadget to your ear. It may sting a little bit, but we can make that better. Just take a big breath for me and hold it until I tell you to let it out, okay?"

I take a big, slow breath in and hold it. The lady puts a metal gun-looking thing to my ear.

"Ready? 3, 2, let out your breath."

I hear a punching noise, but I feel nothing. She puts the metal thing to my other ear and has me take another big breath in.

"One more time. 3, 2, let out your breath."

I hear the punch then feel the sting she told me about. It feels like the time my oldest brother pinched my arm, except my ear feels warm. I reach for my ear, and Mom pushes my hand down.

"Don't touch it, baby girl. You don't want it to get infected," she says.

The lady grabs a mirror and shows me that the little flowers are in my ears like her spikes.

Mom says, "You look so grown up and pretty!" Then she looks at the lady and asks, "Can we pay now? We need to get going."

As we walk out of the store, I ask, "Can we PLEASE stop to see Santa now?"

"No, we have to get you to your dad's," she says as she pulls me away toward the parking lot.

## THIRD GRADE

My storms are as loud as a whisper
I think my teacher sees it
My report card says
"Kelsey is quiet and helpful in class.
But she will have to have extra effort at home to learn.
Please assist her in doing so."

I wonder if he's trying to teach my parents too
I wonder if he knows they don't read his reports
I wonder if he knows I'm quiet
because I'm ready for their forecast
I wonder if he knows how tightly I hold my stuffed bear
when their thunder shakes my walls each night
I wonder if he knows I'm quiet
because their rain muted me

I wonder if he knows I try to splash
in the puddles that I create
every day as I walk to school
So that I can keep my storms
as loud as a whisper
in his classroom

## CHOOSING TO FIGHT

As a teenager
I crafted a mask to look whole
I glued on rhinestone eyebrows
and painted orange smile lines
with yellow dimples that said

*Welcome I understand you*

I knew to fill in my resentful
forehead creases and cracked ears

I saw others breaking
and the avalanches they incited
so I protected my face
into one fit for any climb
I saw my peak hundreds of miles up
and away

I was a messenger drained
A mediator failed

Yet
I decided to fight for my peak
and hoped for a maskless breath

# [Written at 16]

I've lost my breath in the walls
of someone else's home
Spent too much of it fogging windows
and drawing maps of what I imagine
lives beyond behaving
beyond peacekeeping
beyond this house

I'm ready to create my own peace
I've earned my breath

## Atelophobia

Fear of Imperfection

I'm not afraid of dying from
the cancer that ceased my mother's existence
and temporarily ailed my father

I am afraid of dying with
a lackluster contentment
for a life lived in routine
with a man who only made me mostly happy
of settling for mediocrity
when exceptionality was possible

I'm not afraid of the view from the top
or the exhaustion it takes to get there
But of the descent that comes
from looking over too far
towards the pavement
full of failed attempts at perfection

I'm not afraid
of being disappointed
but of being a disappointment
Not of being alone        replaced        or forgetful
but of being lonely        replaceable        and forgettable

I'm not afraid of dying
but of only nearly living

## LEARNED INSTINCT

I have contorted myself enough
to know how my neck and kneecaps
should curl to take up as little space
as a disappearing act allows
It's somewhere between
question mark and whiskey pour spout
(and by space I mean existence)
because taking up
space used to
equate with
being in
the way

I know how to avoid mess
and remove attention
(by mess I mean existence)
See it's no crumbs on plate
to hide residue from judging eyes
because those eyes only saw flaw

I have learned to quiet like mime
with helium in my heels
and mute in my voice box
to remain unheard
because the heard always brought chaos
(and by heard I mean the existing)

So I let closed doors and headphones
become my bunker from the
b e l l o w s
and drywall holes (and by bellows I mean *their* existence)
while blankets of unwashed shaking
became depression holders
and secret keepers that hid my
car-keyed forearms and question mark body
(and by unwashed shaking I mean the pitifulness
I thought *my* existence was worth until I almost let it all go)
until I almost let it all go

# UNDER[CARE]TAKER

Being everyone else's caretaker
makes me my own undertaker
and I'm tired of knowing death

# CHECKLIST CHILD

I am the child you don't have to worry about
Translation: I am the child you don't think about
the one you don't talk about
don't ask about
I followed your rules to avoid your trouble
and became your afterthought child

Achieving dreams yet I'm still a box to check
a Facebook post proving you have a good kid
leaving your indifference out of the caption

The painful part is not
feeling like the checklist child
or crying mascara off in the shower
within 30 minutes of you driving away
with my attachment issues in your trunk
hoping a loofa will scrub off the loneliness
you left for me

The painful part is not
sobbing on my bed with a Spotify playlist
or my childhood blanket being the only hug
available to me in the aftermath

The painful part is not
feeling so unknown that there's no one ready
to catch me how I need after you leave
or feeling so alone that there's no one
I can ask for it from

The painful part is
posting on Facebook and
telling people our visit
was good

## THE ENNEAGRAM TELLS ME I AM NOT A 9

I hear that my war is over
I am no longer peacekeeping the angry
No longer passing by my needs
for the sake of the household
No more fear of pushing someone away

If they can't support my needs
they didn't belong in my home to begin with

# TRIGGER WARNINGS

## MEMORY: 12 YEARS OLD

Dad and I get in his minivan. He's taking me to dance class tonight, though I'm on autopilot. He backs out of the driveway and looks at my face. We drive for a block without speaking.

My mind is silent. My eyes are unfocused. My heart is lead.

"What's wrong?" he asks.

I tune into his voice. Hold my breath.

I say, "I don't want to be sent away to Mom's like the boys were."

My two older brothers got into trouble and were sent to live with Mom. I don't like Mom's house. It's dark, loud, infested, and smells rotten.

"I won't let that happen," he says.

He turns right, and we drive in silence to the dance studio. I count the trees as we pass and let my breath out.

## POETIC TRIGGER WARNING

Dear friend
I know there will be a time when my lack of thought
will make you rightfully angry with me

But when that happens
I beg of you
Please do not come at me yelling

It breaks the white noise I created in my head
to drown the screaming
I grew up hearing

Like the sound of 13-year-old underfed
and over-drunk delinquents and punks
who found refuge
in my momma's closed-curtain living room
You know the ones
who shield any real emotion by trying to be the one
who sounds the angriest
and the most street
because their mommas couldn't pull through for them
and their daddies were either locked up or locked out

My white noise drowned the screaming
I grew up hearing

Like the sound of a 55-year-old stepfather
kicking his dog across the kitchen
as if it was her fault his paycheck stopped growing
You know the one
whose fuse depended on
    the football score
    and which of us kids were around
If we were lucky
the team would win
and we'd get a quiet dinner that night

Please do not come yelling at me
It sets off the smoke detector I installed
to remind myself it was safer to lie
still on the basement couch and take up negative space
than to show myself in the swinging range upstairs

It was safer to listen to the screams and grunts
through the rotting rafters
and tell myself it was just the TV turned up really loud
to tell myself I was safer staying mute
to tell myself I was safe
I was safe
I was safe
I was safe

Friend
if you forget my poetic trigger warning
It's okay
I just wanted you to know
why I might
cover my ears

## Explaining my PTSD

*People with PTSD may have strong negative reactions to something as ordinary as a loud noise or an accidental touch.*[1]

Loud noises meant anger and danger
So she'd wager her rage with her cage
to the beat of the disruption
to avoid a ruptured disruptor

[1] *https://www.psychiatry.org/patients-families/ptsd/what-is-ptsd*

## GRITTY RHYTHM

This is my art and it is dangerous
Imagination formed in trauma
tastes like artificial sweetener
as poems memorialize the bullshit and visceral
I'm shattering the guilty
against their nicotine walls
for leaving me unwashed and blotched

This art tastes like secondhand smoke
My pages reveal realities of those who believed
I'd never speak of the dingy basement couch beds
full of crickets that leapt across my calves
They believed I was youthfully unaware
of their drunken grimaces and prescription abuse
But I'm igniting truths in their kerosene toy boxes

This art is a dangerous unraveling
of self sabotage in closed-curtain living rooms
swallowing dust and musty air freshener
I'm constructing nests of catharsis fit for a mic
forcing the damned to relive
their surround-sound belly screams and belt threats

Those who dared to torment my psyche will
feel my gritty rhythms
and exposure on every stage possible
because I have shred those curtains with the
knives they let rust in the unwashed dishes

They cannot touch me now
They can only hear me now
This is my art
and it is dangerous

# DEAR EX-STEP FATHER

Do you remember when I was 12
and you took the milk gallon from me
while I was carrying it in
telling me it was too heavy for me
and I needed to let the boys carry
the heavy groceries inside
Did you know
that moment created
the independent woman I am now

Did you know
your inability to see my strength
created a lifetime of never asking for help
and proving to everyone how capable I am

Do you wish you could know
who I've grown up to be
Do you wish you could see the woman
you had a sloppy hand in raising

Did you know I became a poet
Did you know I write about you often
Did you know I have a poem coming out soon
about you and your new daughter
Could you do me a favor
Could you read it to her for me

Do you think you can handle it
Do you think you'll learn something along the way
Do you think you'll apply that lesson
and give your do-over a fighting chance

I hope so
at least
for her sake

## TO THE NEW DAUGHTER OF MY EX-STEPFATHER

I hope he has learned the power a young girl holds
tells you you're strong enough to carry the milk gallon
not his anger
says you are just as capable as your brothers

I hope he teaches you to play the banjo
and lets you jam with him
I hope you learn to handle pain
with him            not because of him
I hope you learn faithfulness and patience from him
not in spite of him
I hope you never see a glimpse of his cruelty
and you get to watch him love    just       your mom

I hope his 66 years taught him enough to not screw up
his carbon copy do-over

## THINGS I'VE LEARNED BY REREADING TEXTS WITH YOU, MOM, FROM BEFORE YOU DIED

I've learned I didn't respond enough
I've learned you never had good advice
I've learned you missed out on more than I realized
and that you were desperate
to know who your daughter was
and that you didn't know anything about her
until two months before you left

I've learned you believed I was unaware
of how little money we had
I've learned you were unaware
I was eating as little as possible
        so you could have leftovers when I left

I've learned you were lost in a life
you didn't plan for at 18
that's why you couldn't stop yourself after saying
"I can't believe I'm going to ask my daughter this but..."
followed by your self-deprecation
and inability to see anything good
other than my willingness to treat you
to a venting session

I see now that I was exhausted
and stopped paying attention
I see now that I missed your screams for help
tucked behind silent unclear texts
The last text I got from you was illegible
too many drugs in your system
too little water
too little nutrients
too much heavy
too far past giving up

I see it now
I see it now
I see it now

I feel it now
I feel it now
I feel now
I can feel now

I feel
                    angry

Mom

I've learned I too was forced into a life
I didn't plan for at 18
I've learned I was not born to be your therapist
It was never my job
I've learned I was never a child to you
I was your crutch
your stable one
your trophy to show the world
I've learned it was never my responsibility

I remembered you knew what poetry was for me
You called it my comfort food
and my home to feel peace

You said that I may have been hurt
but at least it gave me something to write about

I've learned you didn't realize
I'd write about
you the most

# 29 : 29 :: Victim : Healing

Today I am 29
the same age you were
in the photo of us dressed in all leather
with dimple grins ready to celebrate
my seventh birthday

At 29
you had nicotine teeth
faded eyes and three kids
7 8 10

You were growing up with us
still learning lessons
we shouldn't have had to watch
finding love in the fists of men
who blamed you for their mayhem

At 29
I have coffee teeth
living eyes and chosen family
312 miles west of that photo

I'm still growing and unlearning
addictions and victimness you taught us
finding love in my own hands
training them in therapy

Mom
it's been 8 years since you won your battle
of trying to leave us without willingly leaving us
I understand now that
after 9 years of waiting
and letting it live for you
you didn't think the cancer was taking you
fast enough

So you stopped drinking water
Let the cola and coffee give
your kidneys permission to kick
because you couldn't see your kids
who chose lives away from you

At 29
I have calculated all my reasons
to stick around
wishing you could've seen them too

But I can't be mad at you for giving up
I can imagine the exhaustion
of pushing pills
two times a day every day
of counting pennies and prescription receipts
month after month
of living as a housebound vagabond
year after year
the defeat in a body unable to travel or work
the loneliness of a resentful husband

I don't know what life was like for you
but I can imagine

I would've wanted to leave too

# KIND OF LIKE LIDOCAINE

I was 5 years old playing with my two older brothers
on the apartment complex playground
It was a downpour and we were sliding and dancing
in the mud full of childhood joy
That was the last memory I have where I felt like a child
That was the last memory I have of us three kids
as a unit

My therapist asks how I feel sharing that story with her
And I say
Kind of like I understand why
I always want to play in the rain
Kind of like I wish I knew what good things happened
 between then and now
Kind of like I'm grieving siblings I never actually lost
 while their ghosts smile at me in photos pretending the hits
 don't exist
Kind of like I can't logic my way out
of how fucking sad it is
 to not have a good memory
 with your brothers in 25 years
Kind of like numbing myself out of this heaviness
and so I do
I fade my eyes out
remove all emotion
as she describes dissociation
and finishes our session

On my way home
I scrape my hand on a door hinge
I let it bleed and bubble until finally rinsing it off
Because isn't that just like me
 to prefer dealing with damage I can bandage

As I wrap the cut I think of how
no amount of gauze can clot their neglect
No cast can mend the brokenness in this family
There is no ointment capable of curing the years

that they disowned me
There was no drug left untested as they searched bottles
        for a sister they left back on that playground
There is no antibiotic for this kind of healing
        so I studied how to inject my own kind of lidocaine
        to avoid it all
and I got good at it

There is a calmness in the numbness
a simple path to breathing and surviving
But I've learned that this numbness shows itself more
        as a lack of joy than a lack of sorrow

So I return to therapy
with a bandaged hand and a raw heart

I ask her to teach me how to stay present
even in the heavy
so that I may finally hold on
to a good memory

# Indifference was distance

My brain mutes when talking about my older brothers
As if they disappeared
from the karaoke nights and road trips
The muddy night playing in the rain-soaked jungle gym
lost its laughter
and the birthday songs and video games were silenced

Our screaming matches
door slams and wall holes
became silent films
Our arguments over Messenger
became cleared notifications

My brain mutes
when trying to be angry resentful or sad with them
As if the choking was playful
indifference was distance
and felonies weren't our headlines

My brain has gone mute writing this poem
I wish it knew I can handle it now
I don't need the protection anymore
I'm capable of moving past it

Unless it knows better than I do

## ETCH-A-SKETCHING MUSCLE MEMORY

*The setting: I'm 28 at my favorite coffeehouse with my poetry family reading a Humans of New York Facebook post. I'm triggered.*

I can feel the edge of tables cracking against skin
hands branding me property
I thought brothers were supposed to protect sisters

My bones vibrate in waves of crickets
and bathtubs trying to etch-a-sketch muscle memory
still holding onto our mother's stale
basement couch never fit for a child's bed
Yet you seemed to enjoy her corrupt walls
and disowned me for not converting to her addictions

I try to dissolve back to the coffeehouse
Not her house
the coffeehouse
Not her house
but chairs scrape the shop floor
my neck flinches to the side
while my eyes burn with the end of your cigarettes
as your vodka removes my eyeliner

She spent every other court-mandated weekend
proving herself party parent
and you fed into her bottles
wrapped your callous fingers around my throat
deemed me unworthy of being sibling
and stopped saying goodbye each time I left

I try to dissolve back to the coffeehouse
Not her house
the coffeehouse
Not her house
but wind slams the shop doors
and my shoulders tighten upright
while the blood in my arms ignite with your lighter

as—A hand touches mine and my eyes
tighten around a freeze response

I try to dissolve back to the coffeehouse
Not her house
the coffeehouse
Not her house
I hear blender Not
bellow
Laughter Not
scream

The hand softens
and I dissolve
to chosen family
bringing me back
to our coffeehouse

# NOISE CANCELLATION

*Dissociation is when, instead of staying present in the face of stress, you exit your thoughts, feelings, and bodily sensations and zone out.*[1]

Chosen family at a coffee shop starts talking louder and louder / Inner me panics / We're going to get in trouble / So I separate myself from the disruption

Fix eyes on table
Board eyes in place
Blur faces and coffee cups until they are staticky
Muffle surrounding people until they are mute
Have no thoughts
Feel comfort in stillness

Replay *Gilmore Girls* in your head
never a full scene though
Skip around

Season 1 episode 17:
RORY: I'm ready to wallow now
LORELAI: [lays pillow on lap,
has Rory lay her head down, dials phone] Hi Joe,
it's Lorelai. I need a pizza with everything, thanks.

Forget where you are
Find blankness behind your pupils
Focus on noise cancellation
Cower into your chest

Season 6 episode 9:
[Lorelai and Rory hug each other
in the lawn]
RORY: I love you, mom.
LORELAI: Aw kid. You have no idea.

Check back in
See if disruption has faded
Softly shake your head to make your eyes move again
Subtly glance around
Hope no one noticed

Check watch to see how much time passed
Be grateful for your new record
only five minutes

# I HAVE AN UNHEALTHY RELATIONSHIP WITH THE WORD DISRUPT

Verb
Used with an object
Definition: to cause disorder or turmoil

I think this is because the disruptive damaged
my childhood into disorder

Disrupt
Verb
Often used with an object

Like a wooden chair in the air
from a broken man behind his curtains

I mean
the object of a sentence
Definition: to cause disorder or turmoil

Like learning to gulp back cry sounds
on the shoulder of my pillow
so I wouldn't disrupt the disruption
at the end of the hallway

Disrupt
Verb
Used with an object

like the brick a broken boy threw
at the neighbor in the second floor window

I mean
the object of a sentence
Definition: to cause disorder or turmoil

Like learning to avoid turbulent turmoil
through muteness and compliance

I have an unhealthy relationship with the word

Disrupt

Verb<br>Used with an object of a sentence<br>Definition: to break apart or radically change

I didn't know radical change
until I was 28 when I learned I never correctly named it
Learned positive disruption can look like
running to a life in minivans and basements
like growing in worn-down shoes and new cities
like projecting my voice to people willing to listen
like writing this poem
when all I ever knew was

Disrupt

Adjective<br>Definition: broken apart

## SIBLINGSHIP

In an alternate universe
the three of us hug     laugh   sip coffee on the patio
catch up on the week behind us and make plans for dinner
We drive to Grandma's together
talking about your date from last week
and a variation I made to Mom's pasta salad

Instead I message you two on Facebook
to ask how your lives have been
this past year

We share the bullet points
and call it a siblingship
    you're sober                    again
    you're starting a new job       again
    I started therapy               again

In an alternate universe
I text you on my lunch break
to ask how your interview went
and you invite me to celebrate over dinner
Then we spend the weekend helping
the other pack and move

Instead shared trauma separates us
further than the states between unfamiliar homes
And I know I'm holding the door closed
but your welcome stayed behind when I freed myself
from being your mediator and now
I only remember you exist when someone asks how you are
because pieces of my memory
are hiding in boxes stored in the basement
of each home we lived in

In an alternate universe
the three of us hug     cry     sip coffee at Grandma's table
reminiscing on singing with Mom and hearing her cackle
We drive to the cemetery together

talking about our last visits with her
and a plan to see each other again next week

Instead
You ride alone
I ride with dad
and you show up late
We hug goodbye
and say
we'll check in

# To my Older Brothers

I don't have to remind you
that most of the doors you've chosen
were spiked and crusted
leading you to bottles and bail bonds but

I hope each view faded
the green you sought into
art fit for a family wall

Though we don't really know what family means
do we

Digits do not exist for how
often the two of you told me
your eyes did not hold me as a sister
so I hope you understand why I left
you alone with your doors and
chose my own with grass
you could not see
because your indifference turned away
my plea for a family
But we don't really know
what family means
Do we

To my older brothers
I need you to understand that I had
become the ashes of every wish
our mother made for you
Taking the textbook path to standard success
The kind parents didn't worry about
          or notice
While you forged paths of crime and neglect
The kind parents worry about
          and notice

I became a tunneled candle
unable to care for itself long enough to stay alive
Too busy throwing our family glints of mediation
and attempts at peace restoration
But we don't know what family means

So you let divorce and addiction create
decades of sibling separation and
you sealed it
with our mother's final door

# I Go Back to November 15, 2014

My past self leaves the ICU and my current self appears
  not quite a ghost
  more like a thought

I hear my brother talk of leaving Momma's bedside
I want to tell him to stay
  He will regret everything he is about to do
I want to say Please
  Help her brush her hair
  Paint her nails
  Sing with her
  Sit with her
  Do everything you said I wouldn't have to
    worry about if I left to get some sleep

I see him stand up
I want to push him back down
  Take his keys from the table
  drug money from his pocket
Tell him she won't be here tomorrow
Tell him he will ruin the next ten years of his life
Tell him of the cells he will see
  the children he will neglect
  the hearts he will numb
  the family wall he will be removed from
Tell him he will lose me as a sister in about two days
and he will never truly reconnect with our brother

But I don't

I want the path I take
more than I want a better one for him

I see him step to the table
I move his keys closer to his hand
and let him fuck it all up

# STARTING OVER

# MEMORY: 19 YEARS OLD

**7:12 a.m.**
STOMP STOMP STOMP STOMP echoes through the unfinished ceiling above my bed. I slept maybe four hours all night, and the last thing I need is my little half-brother jumping around above me.

STOMP STOMP STOMP. I feel my skin start to roast. This has happened every morning this week. I'm exhausted. I wish my step mom would do something to make him stop.

STOMP STOMP.

"SHUT UP!!!!" I yell as my fuse bursts.

STOMP.

I fling out of bed and up the basement stairs. He runs to his room.

"I'm so tired of this!" I yell to my step mom in the kitchen.

"I'm not going to keep him quiet so you can sleep all day!" She yells.

I run back downstairs and slam my door. I flop on my bed and pull the blanket over my head. I start sobbing. *What about me? What about what I need? And I don't sleep all day. Maybe ask me why I can never get out of bed until 10 a.m.*

**7:25 a.m.**
After ten minutes, I hear the garage door open. She's taking him to preschool. She'll be gone about twenty minutes, half an hour max. I could get a little more sleep.

But I see my hamper of clean clothes, backpack, and dance bags. I feel something switch and my body becomes its own. My arms add regular shoes and a coat to my dance bag. I stuff as many other clothes as possible into the hamper. I toss my journal and as many books as I can fit into my backpack.

My legs run outside and pull my minivan into the driveway. Then they run back downstairs. I feel my hands throw bags on my shoulders and lift my hamper. I throw as much as I possibly can fit into the van. Fill it with bags, clothes, blankets, and the few stuffed animals I feel attached to. The doors close, and I run back downstairs.

I look around and see there's still a lot in here but nothing that I need.

My hands write a note. I say things I never imagined writing or speaking into existence. My hands crumple it into my pocket and decide against leaving it.

I'm running out of time.

I grab my keys. Walk upstairs and into the garage. Sit in my driver's seat. Close the garage. Start the engine. And for the first time, I see why I was meant to own this van.

**7:45 a.m.**
I back out of the driveway and start driving.

My switch turns off, and I realize, I don't have a plan.

*Oh shit. Where do I go? I don't have anywhere to live. What did I just do? I can't take it back now. She's probably almost back to the house already. She'd see me bringing it all back in. I'm in this now.*

I drive to the one place I've been finding comfort lately. The park on the edge of town with the deer sanctuary.

I sit in the parking lot and cry. I let 19 years of suppression soak my face. I text my current best friend.

**8:30 a.m.**
"I need help. I have nowhere to go."

He calls me, "What's going on? Where are you?"

I explain everything.

“Let me ask my grandma if you can stay with us. One second,” he hangs up.

I look around at the park. It looks different somehow. Not mine. Not my swings, not my street, not my town. Not anymore. I feel the weight of the step I just took, and I take as many deep breaths as I can. I breath in and hold it. Then tell myself, *3, 2, let your breath out.*

He calls me back, “Grandma said you can stay in the basement here. We can make it so you have your own area. You don’t have to pay rent, just buy your own groceries, and do your own laundry and dishes.”

—

I don’t hear from my family for a of couple weeks. Dad finally texts me asking if we could meet up for lunch. So, I go, holding my breath.

“Will you come back home? I miss having you around,” he asks. His eyes are genuine.

*3, 2, let your breath out.*

“I can’t do that,” I say.

## WHAT THEY DON'T TELL YOU ABOUT RUNNING AWAY

There will be no plan
no intention to leave
It'll just          happen
The silence will break
          and so will you

There will be no montage
no soundtrack to your packing or driving
no side character helping you leave and
no end credits signaling a happy ending

There will be no mirror waiting for you
no dresser          no bed
Just a pull-out couch
and sheets hanging from rafters
creating a room in your friend's grandma's basement

There will be no contact
for the first two weeks
You will not know if they notice the empty floor
or if they wonder where your van has been sleeping

There will be lunch                    at a Burger King
and this will be the scene you remember most
Because there will be no relief in your father's eyes
when he asks you to come back
But there will be peace in yours

because there will be no returning

## BREATH IN A HOME

There's freedom in running away
in moving and leaving them behind

My third-generation-hand-me-down minivan
valeted my baggage
from family basement to friend's couch

Air moves through my lungs
for the first time after 19 years
of secondhand smoke and bearing parental weight

The expansion in my ribs heals and deepens
with each year that passes

Safety welcomes my breath
in a home I've nested and
I'm no longer holding it in

They can't hear me anymore
can't look for me anymore
can't guilt me anymore
They gave up

I exhaled

## [Written at 20]

I boarded this train 20 years ago
I've bumped and rattled along with it
Never straying from the tracks
I've broken down with mechanical problems
gotten stuck waiting for freight trains to pass
been nervous traveling over rivers and bridges
and felt like I'd never see the other side of the steep hill

But now I'm beginning to see the train station
I'm almost free to walk the Earth as I please
with the bumps of the train engraved in my every step
making me a stronger person altogether
After 20 years of riding someone else's track
it's my time to walk my own path

## GOALS OF GALAXIES

With goals far from the Milky
I find a Way
to steer myself through
the stepping stars
around meteors

And though it will take light years
I will not settle among
the familiar system
because I'm shooting for galaxies
not just stars

## TREE OF WEEDS

She was put into a family tree
with withered leaves and torn branches
a tree that really isn't a tree
because it's really more like a bush or a lawn full of weeds
just trying to look like they're flowers
and this poor dandelion's head popped off

Her pollen blew across the yard
past the oak tree full of healthy leaves
and the tulips waving their perfect colorings
as she tumbled forward through the wind
who pushed back trying to restrain her from replanting
    in an unapproved field because
    why would she want to grow somewhere new
    why would she think she's capable of being
    anything else
    why would she get it in her head
    that being a weed is only surface level

Well somewhere along the line she decided
that she refused to be like them

She knew she had more to her
than being a parasite on an unwelcoming lawn
She knew someday she'd land in a field
and find herself a strong seed
that would grow with her into a real tree

One that thrives from the soil
appreciates the sun and gives oxygen
Not one that takes nutrients
gets mad when the sun is too close
and fails its counterparts

Because
somewhere along the line
she realized she was capable of being
anything      else

## How far I've come

Some look at my life and say
I know how to keep busy

I look at my life and say
I know how to keep from falling
back to the depths of night skies
that stole my desire for growth

## Cafephobia

Fear of coffee

Aren't I just like this dusty coffee pot
abandoned on a screened-in porch

out of place

with the fingerprints of those
who closed me off to freshness

Maybe they brought me here to enjoy with the view
Maybe they believed I never made the roast just right

So they left me neglected
with a muffled reflection

Never took time to let me try again
to be what they needed

They never put grounds in me
in the first place

It was never my fault

## AUTOPHOBIA

FEAR OF BEING ALONE

Loneliness is counting hangers
in your open closet until you
see the one that's missing the sweater you haven't found

Loneliness is the nauseating hunger
that comes a couple hours after
indulging in orange chicken and Dr. Pepper

It's identifying with the one burnt-out bulb
on a 12-foot strand of Christmas lights
that none of the other bulbs seemed to notice

Loneliness is a glass of scotch on the rocks
minus the scotch
and the rocks

It's sitting at a bar after your first paid gig
with the empty scotch glass
and no one you love around you

It's writing a new stanza
every time you try to fall asleep
at 11:30 2:45 4:00

It's finally falling asleep
but waking up holding your laptop

Loneliness is seeing your mother
sleep alone in a bed
with her husband by her side

Loneliness is just a word
and I am its embodiment

## ASKING FOR HELP: AN OPEN LETTER

hi

it's me
i know we haven't spoken in a while
and i also know that it's my fault

you see
i've been held captive by an enemy
as alluring as a siren
and as resilient as the rocks that sink them

i've gotten good at using
a makeshift raft while drowning
my voice instead of asking for help
because i thought it burdensome and selfish

i know now
the raft was only an open door not quite heavy enough
to keep me from becoming a forgotten Titanic passenger

i know now
that it's okay to ask
to be loved a little bit extra
on days i forget how to love myself

but i need you to know
somedays i need you without being asked
because my voice can get carried into the whirlpool
that leaves me silently gasping

i need you to know
i love you

but mostly
i need you to know that
i need you
always
and right now

## Ode to Sylvester

Let your minivan hug you through the heavy
He'll store your history and carry you to a new town

driving your unknown until you find a park
far enough away
He'll let you breathe and scream and sing
and hit his steering wheel

He'll do this over and over
while you find home in his doors
and take your shoes off to rest your feet on his floors

He sees you tiptoeing through traumas
and tries to take some of it away
Roll his windows down
He will show you the power of a wind revival
how spring breathes for you and beckons you to its grass
Open his door and run barefoot through your new chance

He'll be there waiting for you
when it's time for your next route
for the change you both know you're ready for

Let his speakers sing you down the highway
to the next state over

He will have many breakdowns
But he will hold you through yours

He has a way of getting you everywhere
that you didn't expect
of cleaning the windshield in time to see your new view

Someday after he's lived his last life
you'll find yourself surrounded
by city glow and falling snow

He got you to the place where you now carry
your notebook to coffee shops and martini bars

the place where you laid him to rest in a ramp
while you explored a life he wanted for you

You will marvel at the way a van taught you
that a city and a decision can change courses

that views and stories can heal heaviness
You will realize he was the vehicle for your past self

to fight for the better version that you're walking in now

# MIRROR-VIEW MAGIC

I spent decades living what I believed they expected
wishing my reflection would suddenly feel familiar
but it was never my mirror to begin with

I spent years biking to the empty elementary school field
growing a pseudo love of expression in isolation
That's what forced me into my packed-up van
that drove me to put the place I knew in my rearview
to find my reflection

I moved myself to a place
where the mirror was harsher
and screaming for Windex

But it was mine
My lonely view of the city
My mattress on the studio floor
My books outnumbering reflections

I moved myself to
clothes-covered floor and shoe-piled doorway
to book-stacked windowsill and dish-full counter

To a studio that taught me to be real
like poetry
and that I'll never be a morning person
but it always had coffee

To a studio that hugged away my scar arms
and taught me to take up space
Taught me to survive loneliness
by counting lights from the rooftop
blurring them into one large stepping stone

It taught me to fill my pages with raw ink
discovering my why
through metaphors and merlot

And my mirror
Well my mirror still needs a frame
and Windex

But at least
it's my mirror

# ODE TO MY BROWN WALMART SANDALS

I know you're worn down
and your sole separation says
I've gotten my money's worth

But the five dollars I spent on you
four years ago
is nothing compared
to the van you bonded with
the planes you've rested on
fountains you've danced in
and cobblestone you've stumbled across

The steps you helped me take
fed my travel bug and carried me
to each new stage when I needed it

Your first year guided me through
the campus library
walking me into potential and degrees
I didn't know existed

You rode on trains and buses around our country
then flew with me across the pond
to teach me there are no boundaries
in possibility and adventure

The year after
your lack of tread danced on sticky bar floors
and late night asphalt
reminding me to soak in the moments
with people I'll never forget

You hugged me through the breakup that broke me
trying to prove some things can last
You stuck to my feet
as I navigated a new state
finding my way
alone with you

The year after
Together we learned to say goodbye
to those we danced alongside
and the van who saved us

Together we found poetry stages
where you discovered the comfort of carpet under a mic
freeing me to finally speak

And the year the pandemic hit
you gripped my feet fearing
like all of us
that your time was coming

So you skipped with me as my new love proposed
You toured our first home with us
and walked me into the safety you knew I'd find

When he and I began unpacking our boxes
you took one last walk around the block
let your straps give way
and reminded me
how to say goodbye

# FROM SYLVESTER TO NIGEL

Hold her safely in your seats
as she surrounds herself with your cool air

She needs you to store her life in your trunk for a while
I promise she will love you as if you're her person

She didn't expect to end up back in a packed-up car
sitting in a park with nowhere to go

She didn't expect to be alone again
She will lean her grief and relief on your headrest

Let her turn your volume up as high as it goes
It's the only release she has right now

If she hits your dash
know that she's not hitting you

If her eyes stop moving
know that they're too sore from carrying

her heart through yet another heavy year
Remind her she is safe with you

and that you will carry her
to wherever she wants to exist next

# UNFINISHED

Aren't we all just drafts
wishing the next struggle will be the revision
we need      so we can see the poem
      we're trying to be

When we see our poem
we'll edit parts we thought finished
but revealed            outdated
We'll shape them
until consonants      become music
      vowels turn to art
and pauses            create silent dances

We'll edit
and watch our poem
                              write itself

# EXITING SURVIVAL MODE

# MEMORY: 23 YEARS OLD

August condensation drips off my rocks glass and falls a few hundred feet to the sidewalk. I take a sip of bourbon and admire the city lights below while I sit on my high-rise rooftop. Pride and grief overwhelm me.

*I did it. I got the good job in a new city and a good apartment for my new life. I don't know anyone yet, though. Somehow, I'm sadder than I was before. Shouldn't I be happier than ever? I made it out. Isn't this the happy ending?*

The memory of it all fills my eyes. I breathe back tears.

*3, 2, Let out my breath.*

Let a tear fall.

*At least I made it out.*

## I WISH I DIDN'T RELATE TO THEIR EXHAUSTION

Some articles have shown that
Princess Aurora struggles with depression
and Ophelia struggles with PTSD
and I wish I didn't relate to their exhaustion

I have this fortitude heart
that constantly weaves itself
into some avant-garde herringbone pattern
It does this to appear beautifully stable
as if I'm not delicate
as if I'm not constantly fermenting myself
as if there's not an ongoing kerfuffle between
my inner Aurora and Ophelia
while I hide them under my cardigan
hugging them where no one can see

I wish I didn't relate to their exhaustion

I'm tired of forcing myself to feel
some sort of compersion
for the people blessed with serotonin
The ones happily dancing in bluegrass spaces
The ones with natural pizazz and sonnet smiles

I'm tired of never-ending doubt pouring around my head
while I lay in a chair feeling like a spud
reading articles about princesses
and Shakespeare characters
numbing myself away from the trauma reminders
hoping tomorrow will be the day
I can get myself up again

## THE ANATOMY BEHIND A SELFIE

155 weeks ago
I posted an attempt at self love
It was Valentine's Day after all

The beanie he bought me
made its appearance as if to say
he was still here keeping my mind warm
and the coat he got me
showed off my inability to start fresh

The smile in my cheeks proves I learned
just how tight to pull my mouth back
forcing my dimple out of hibernation
long enough to post a reminder
that I wasn't as alone as my forearms
said I was

My self-love trap's comment section was a shrine
of awe and pride

I didn't share
the brick blotches under my foundation
I became the snow smothering a flower bed
and any sign of real life

# DYSTHYMIA

## PERSISTENT DEPRESSIVE DISORDER

I hold you hostage
in order to push on
toward the safety of my blanket

But it feels like there's a bookshelf
standing from my gut
to my scalp

and its books
progressively
fall
in pairs
I hear
every
page
in its own
breeze
and feel
every
hardback
meet
the floor

Yet holding you hostage
is just as exhausting

as setting you free

# MY BED CALLED ME AGAIN TODAY

For a couple weeks now I've managed to send him to voicemail
See I forced myself outdoors
and let that become the kind of habit people don't question
the kind of habit they say fixes everything in the long-term

I suppose this is why he's been
calling daily
Because I lead him to believe I needed him
daily
And for the longest time I did

I used to answer every call
believing he'd use his synthetic comfort
to make all of it disappear
all the thoughts
resembling cracked spines and cat scratches
flat tires and empty pantries

He did
make all of it disappear
only temporarily

So I tried to go back to life
to ignore his ringing
and search for joy each day

Today though

Today I answered him

Today

I allowed myself to drown
in the wrapping of his sheets and lay
the hammer in my head on his pillows

I let him inside my sinkhole chest and
ignored laundry for
           yet        another            day
My body is exhausted and
pushing him away doesn't seem to bring the long-term any closer
So today
I will let him
try                  to fix               me

## POETS ARE BORN TO BE SAD

My depression looks like<br>
adding clean clothes to the pile of last week's<br>
        and the week's before<br>
        and                before that

It looks like<br>
clean dishwasher becoming counter of<br>
never-made-it-to-cabinet<br>
and gifted books sitting on one another<br>
not ready for shelving<br>
and quick afternoon nap becoming missed dinner

My depression looks like<br>
earbuds at lunch<br>
        and no social media

It's    eyes staring<br>
at mirror in work bathroom<br>
        reminding me to hold it hostage until home<br>
because home means being alone and safe in comforters

It looks like<br>
Christian music on repeat<br>
even though I'm not one anymore<br>
because maybe<br>
He<br>
will still fix me

## Reasons don't always exist

The humidifier in my throat
nails my arms to this desk and my shoulders to the chair
My eyes frantic
hope no coworker sees
my mold of depression
clinging to what little air and motion it finds

5 o'clock greets me like
an acquaintance from high school that I at one point knew
I feel my shell place a bag on my shoulder
slide one foot

after another after another

after another

until I reach the vaguely familiar apartment door
I turn a key
listening to each click say safety is near
I drop the bag and remove shoes
as I curl around a pillow

I let the culmination of pressure points
strap my legs to the mattress
and I welcome the weight of two comforters

# LIVING IN THE FIREPLACE

The hollow in my ribs is screaming tonight
Tells me it will not be silenced
It's done with constant burial
and begs to be acknowledged

It's resurrecting itself
despite all the eulogies I've written for it

For tonight
I will live vicariously through the fireplace
with all its energy and purpose
within its confines
How I wish I felt that heat
Its flames sing hymns
while burning dust
hypnotizing my depression
synthesizing a calm within the motion
as I sink into this couch hugging my hollow
for tonight

# ASSESSING MY DEPRESSION

Dry skin on my ankle bone sheds the shell
I accumulated in isolation and catches on the blanket scratches
that my cat left or maybe it was my untrimmed toenail

My rough fingerprints snag on my unshaven shin
knee and thigh scraped by skin on the side of my thumb
picked back with uncertainty and ragged fingernails

that claw scab spots on my arm and neck Then flatten to palms
trekking through the back of my slimy scalp screaming for help
Begging for attention

## YOU ARE NOT INANIMATE JUST BECAUSE YOU HAVE DEPRESSION

Winter molds your sculpted frame to the desk chair
as your mind maps out small things that can get you moving

Put on slippers // Grab notebook // Write the freeze out // Sip water in cup from yesterday because at least it's water // Take deep breath // Feel water start to thaw your chest into remembering yourself

Let someone you love hug you

Go outside // Take slippers off // Place bare feet on cold concrete // Recognize the difference between your living stature and the inanimate cement // You are not inanimate

Put slippers back on // Walk back inside // Sit back in chair // Take another sip of water // Breathe deep // Remember you deserve warmth

You deserve motion and
You deserve warmth

# My compass

Poetry made itself my compass through the intense
No stanza of mine was written for the simple
Why would they if life never breaks
lines into calm
I am not skilled
at the simple sounds of slow
My pencil has not sharpened
in a soothing sharpener
and my ink only knows
knuckles or nuptials
But I'm ready to know
the in between
How to write the little things
To learn that they're stronger
than the intense
as they welcome me into rest

# Insomnia Spectator

I've been seeing 2:30 a.m. a lot lately
She's become a comfort
a new kind of honest writing hour
She holds my triggers for me
lets me see who I've become despite them
and reminds me I'm still human
figuring all this out

While her ceiling fan noise hugs me to my mattress
reminding me that my thoughts
aren't wrong in the absence of action
they're just thoughts

She teaches me more about myself
than her sister hour knows

## WHISPER APP

It's 2012
I'm 18

*I cut for the first time tonight*
*I'm not crying anymore*

I send this anonymous Whisper
to the comfort of the internet
as I weigh myself down with depressed blankets
in a basement room lightless
The only sound
is my shaking

Life is not deadening
and my car key is more than a road trip
as it etches trauma into my forearms like a map
for anyone who might bother to memorize its path
though no one has memorized my face enough
to notice the tension in my suction cup smile

So I lay here
plucking scabs like violin strings
searching for my final measure
thinking tomorrow I'll add tattoos
so the twinge of skin can be sharper

For now I'll search
and pluck
and think
until the density of depression
shuts me down for the night

It's 2018
I'm 24

*I hurt myself tonight*

I send this knowing text to the one who will call me
as I fall into sobs on a lukewarm bath mat
in a studio lonely for laughter
The only sound
is my phone buzzing on the tile

Life has deadened
My car key doesn't help anymore
and my nails are an okay second choice
since they hold enough of my ruins under their polish
to hide it from anyone who may try to admire the art
but no one has admired my heart long enough to notice
my need for a touch up

So I lay here
listening to my best friend's voice
hugging me across state lines
reminding me I'm finally not alone
helping me see the monuments each of my tomorrows are
as I write my way through this

For now I'll breathe
and think
and create
until the density of depression
lifts for a while

It's 2023
I'm 29

Life has revived
I still pick at scabs but
I hurt myself for the last time five years ago
and I'm not crying anymore

# DERMATILLOMANIA

I have a habit of picking at my shoulder scabs
and nose scar
I think this must be why I'm a poet

I tug at wise wounds until they re-bleed
their truths become a self-regulation tactic
filtering droplets into diatribes and didactics
hoping each re-healing will be my relief
But each re-scabbing reveals my numbing
until emotion itches at the surface
begging me to scrape again

So I start the process over
attempting some poetic understanding
of where the feeling comes from

# CATCH THAT THOUGHT

Loneliness and I have never played well together
And though I know I'm more capable now than last time
of not giving into my harmful ideations
I can still feel the placebo relief they gave me

Instead I will let the tears take their time dripping
while I trace tattoo templates on my forearm
where I want to scrape my nails
because making something beautiful
from my mental health
has always been my strongest suit
and I cannot start back at day zero after six years free

Instead I will sit cross legged
on the corner of my bed
pressing my palms into my arms
frozen in my head
screaming for relief
realizing I forgot this side effect of my loneliness

I will remind myself to look around and find
a blue book, blue note card, blue trophy
green book, green sweater, green leaves outside
cozy blanket, cozy lights, cozy windows

I will remind myself to write this poem
I will want to send it to everyone I love
but will choose not to
They don't need to worry about me

Then I will catch that thought
and do my best to find the ground again
feel the hardwood stick to my bare feet
as I pace myself walking to the kitchen
to sip fresh water and remember
to keep breathing

on my own

# DISSOCIATION EMBODIED

I've never been good at keeping my feet on the ground
always lifting myself out of the uncomfortable
Folding my body into a shape I can control
one I know how to feel

Being grounded was never safe
so I taught myself to contort through traumas
This tool made booths and couches welcoming
gave me something to sit with instead

But now I don't know how to break this habit
how to exist in the uncomfortable
I don't know how to welcome it with two feet on the floor

But I'm trying

# A POEM IN WHICH MY EMOTIONS ARE AT THE DMV AND I AM THE CLERK

I say
Take a number
grab a seat
please be patient with me
I know I've worked here for 30 years
but this is my first day with so many of you at once
and I have no help anymore
just the lessons I learned in training

Now serving ticket number Depression
who slumps in the chair at my desk
says she's not quite sure why she's here today
but she knows she must keep me company
She won't leave my chair
tells me to drag another emotion up
and keep going through the line

I grab my phone instead
because I just don't want to be doing this work today
but I see Playful out front giggling to herself as she jumps in front
of the automatic door
having a great time letting the others in first
She says she will only let herself inside once I've handled
everyone else
so I keep going

Now serving ticket number Anxiety
who walks up with Insecurity by her side
They printed every possible form
but aren't sure which ones they need
I take a breath and calmly ask them questions
gentle parenting them long enough to realize
they don't need to be here
everything is actually okay
I send them away

Now serving ticket number Annoyance
who got carded at the bar with an expired license then learned she can't renew it online
so she was forced to come in here and deal with others

Responsible spends the wait studying for her CDL
not because she needs one but just in case she has to step in for someone else again

Uncertainty applies for a job
any job

Optimism just left with the ride-share service seeking sunshine she knows she won't see here

Resentment is still 16 and ready to take her road test
to leave her hurt behind
and release herself with the windows down

Grief and Love fill out updates
to their emergency contact info

Lonely is still at the kiosk
waiting for it to give her a number

Yet after all of this
Playful has not come inside
She's still having fun at the door

I look around to see who I missed and realize
Joy and Anger are nowhere to be seen
I believe they're sitting at home filling out online forms
hoping one day I can give them the attention they need

I take a break and call them up
tell them they are welcome here now
I am making space in this office
and I want to meet them
Both of them
I know how to feel them now
even with all the others here

Joy is ecstatic and hops in her car right away
Knows she has been preparing for this day all our life
Anger is scared
Knows she is untrained
but believes I can help her learn
so she makes her way here
cautious

They walk in together
help Lonely get her ticket
grab their own
and take their seats

Now serving tickets Joy and Anger
I ask why they are together
and why they never came to the DMV before
They say they are the extremes
They've been waiting for me
to allow myself to feel everything else
They say the longer I numbed myself
the less chance they had at getting to the front of the line

I apologize
give them a hug
ask them to stick around and get to know the others

Then I notice
Playful skipping inside
taking her number
saying I'm ready for another day at my DMV

# WELCOME TO MY CONCINNITY

Welcome to my concinnity
Watch as I skillfully piece myself together
and become a stunning start-over
Watch as I put in the work to heal
    everything that has hurt me since I was toddler

See I was always limited on liquidity
The assets I was dealt never quite made
my life ends meet
    I was always falling short
    of receiving attention while
    following rules meant to keep me
    as they needed me
    Rules like start paying my dues at 15
    and never bring up the receipts
    like be available without notice and fill their roles
    Like mediate don't instigate
    and stay hidden unless needed
Two decades of paying rent on these rules drained me
So I'm going into my thirties building my own

Watch as I become a lichen
as the parts of me that are still living
merge into a healed version
A version that left those sycophants behind
They can't benefit from this kind of evolution
They don't get to dictate the rules I live by
They don't get to ask me for anything anymore
They only have karma to answer to
    and so do I
My karma is a Chanel smile
It's showing itself as a life of luxuries I never knew
like joy and safe people
like becoming whole and bright
like being rich in fulfillment

I invite you to watch my healing as you please
Might I recommend grabbing your pen

and a pair of sunglasses
You'll want to take notes but this is a supernova spotlight
My past has died and its light burns
with an intensity only seen in healthy boundaries
and setting up a life away from the outdated rules

I invite you to watch my healing as you please
I only ask that you call me Dua Lipa
because I've got New Rules for a life without regrets

So welcome to my concinnity
May you learn something along the way
May I live as a reminder that you too can put in the work
    that you too can heal into your own rules
    and that you too can skillfully piece yourself together

# BEING OKAY

# MEMORY: 30 YEARS OLD

It's 1:00 in the morning. Dad and I are standing in his kitchen. He's finishing the beer he nursed as we talked, and I'm finishing a canned cocktail while laughing at a joke he just made.

"So, we always talk about how they're doing and wondering if they're okay," he says. "But are *you* okay?"

I hold my breath, trying to remember a time anyone in the family had asked me that.

*3, 2, let out my breath.*

"I am, actually."

## TO MY YOUNGER BROTHERS

At not quite 1 and 5 years old
I wanted you to play and laugh

I tended your needs as best I could
while I hid a depression so rooted in my own childhood

it carved out my starving cheekbones
I tried to navigate door after door
and lost myself in the maze

I hope you feel my heart
hugging you through the screen

Showing you a life you may not see
lived in front of you

I hope you learn the distance I hold
means you still have me around

I had to leave to keep myself
above ground

To my younger brothers
I hope you learn the doors you see in front of you

may not be the ones to choose
sometimes the best ones are dust-covered

with a knock only you can hear

# DEAR FROG AND TOAD,

*It's been a while since I last saw you two, and I know that was my doing. Would you like to join me for a fresh cup of coffee tomorrow morning? We can meet at the park on top of the hill like we used to and chat.*

*Your old friend,*
*Kelsey*

I walk to the park and they're not here yet
I sit on the boulder by the river
that I once made into a home
My first sip of dark roast
goes straight to the soul I believed I wasn't worth
and have finally replanted

This park looks the same
I see the patch where
neglect and moss globbed me to the hill
while flies nested in my unkempt hair
forcing me to sit with my lonely
making friends with a frog and a toad

I take a few more sips and remember
the open field nearby
where they gave me warts
and taught me that
flying a kite can be chaotic
others will scoff at your choices
and the two of them would keep me company

Another sip while waiting and I glance at the creek
where they watered my hat in murk
because that was all we had to work with
They helped me believe my mind could grow
though I could only see as shallow as their puddles

The coffee cooled as I sat remembering
when winter settled in
and my friends buried themselves
like snow blankets weighing on me like old habits
Remembering that I stopped visiting the park
after I discovered rivers capable of flowing under ice

Remembering the time I was alone again
when I learned to keep clean hair
and the flies left me alone
when I learned warts and toxic people will fade
if I let them
because moss can't grow if I keep moving

I drink the last of my coffee and realize
the young girl from the park doesn't exist anymore
I haven't needed my old friends in quite some time

I think of them often but I have written new stories
I now breathe by freshwater lakes
I have friends who prefer flying
and I know how to choose my aloneness

I see now that my old friends
prefer flies and murky water
They don't understand clean joy
Maybe they know this too
Maybe they've always known it
Maybe that's why they never showed

## DEAR 15-YEAR-OLD ME

Today is not going to be a great day
It won't be a great week or even next several years
But I need you to eat a full meal once in a while
because disappearing will never be the answer

I need you to be honest with your friends
Tell them what's happening within you
and your heart will lighten with each conversation

I need you to turn the bath water off
let your lungs re-meet fresh air
and dry off the pity you're hiding in your throat
There are clear breaths waiting for you if you keep trying

I need you to remember your car key
is not meant to etch trauma maps into your forearms
Please keep turning to your notebook instead
I promise I will thank you for writing through it all

I need you to know your picture smile will become real
It's going to take longer than you've asked of that wishing star

But I need you to know
that each light you've watched fall
has built you a sky of glimmers
and you will learn to connect them
into constellations
glowing on your face

## SPROUTING

I've never known the love of a family
where the deeply personal bonds you

in ways only branches can hold
I see now that the tree I've planted

is sprouting green leaves
with each fact we share

I'm learning family trees
are built in roots of trust and time

## LAUGH-OUT-LOUD PERSON

I am not a laugh-out-loud person
while watching my favorite show

but my partner is a belly laugher
I'm learning it's safe

to enjoy the simple things

## SITTING WITH MY 5-YEAR-OLD SELF:

Little Me sits across the table in this coffeeshop booth. She orders a hot chocolate with whipped cream, and I order a drip coffee.

Her hair is just like mine: long, bright blonde, bangs, a little unruly, but free. She's wearing her favorite yellow *Winnie the Pooh* overalls with a white t-shirt and sneakers.

Little Me giggles when the barista puts her drink in front of her. Her eyes are alive and full of glee. Squinting with a smile, she scoops some whipped cream up. I smile as she gets some on her chin.

I hand her a napkin, and she stops smiling to wipe her face off.

She looks at me as if questioning if I like my drink. I look at my cup of black coffee and sip. It's soothing but bitter.

I sigh and ask the barista for a caramel latte instead. With whipped cream.

Little Me claps when the barista brings me my new drink. She sips her hot chocolate, coming up with a clump of whipped cream on her mouth.

I chuckle and sip mine too.

She laughs with her whole belly when I get whipped cream on my mouth too.

We sit together with silly, messy faces, and we finish our fun drinks together.

## SELF-PORTRAIT

AFTER ASHTON JORDAN

I've been trying to find her again
the girl in the photos
The one who loved cool mornings and swing sets
who caught fireflies
used the world as her jungle gym
and laughed easily

Her hands got cinched
between the office and suburbs
forgetting she never cared about her paycheck
just that she traced the nape of Love's neck
with flower fingers then snatched her notebook
from her purse when the poem appeared

Her feet evaporated in the depressed heat
then floated through an unfamiliar life
of perceived permanence
She forgot she never cared where she was going
just that she would dance on the trails
splash in the lake water on days she need regrounding
then let Love join in her joy

I've been finding her again
the girl in the photos
She was hiding in skyline corners and stage curtains
waiting for me to remember
she was never meant for normality
waiting for me to make the decision
she knew I was ignoring
waiting for me to skip back to the mic with a full heart

I've found her again
the girl in the photos
The one who is admiring fireflies again
who has rediscovered swing sets
and is ready to welcome Love
when they show themself again

I have found myself again
the me from the photos
and I am rebuilding a home
in my smile lines

# When the Map Is No Longer Highlighted in Survival

What do I do after surviving a crosswalk
I spent 29 years building as I crossed
After the snow has settled
the traffic has calmed
and the sun has waved me across the street

What do I do with these painted hands
they never learned how to hold
just to fold my feelings into my pocket
and help others across

These concrete feet haven't learned how to beat
their crust off just to fight off the weight of each year
What do I do when the construction is complete

How do I step on an unfamiliar sidewalk
instead of sticking around to sit in my handiwork for a while
to admire the elbow grease I pushed for
to allow myself a release into a life I fought for
How do I walk on

How do I know which road to follow
when the map is no longer highlighted in survival
I'm learning they call this a revival
and it's my turn to create the paths I discover

I'm no longer taking cover or being pulled into the cracks
And I'm learning the hard hat I crafted
from my own back
never actually fit me
Just enough to look protected

I'm learning to remove it
and let my head breathe sky again
let my hair feel breeze again

I'm learning to let my feelings unfold
especially the good ones
I'm told their names are
Relieved
Peaceful
Fulfilled
Alive
I'm learning that these feelings will live longer
outside of my pocket

I'm learning my crosswalk meant
I built a curbside safe enough to take my first step
as I begin building a sidewalk all my own
one that can hold the weight
of the heavy and the hopeful

# Low-Income Lullaby

Today I realized I cry a lot in grocery stores
Something about the cereal aisle and all its cartoons
They pour me a bowl of suppressed emotions
over a childhood I was never afforded
I clear my throat and ignore the lack of memories

I get to the checkout lane
everything scanned and bagged
Then watch my card decline this week's food
The cashier sees grief filling my eyes
And says he'll worry about putting them back for me
I whisper a thank you and
walk to my car as unnoticeably fast as possible
Sit in my drivers seat and
let the hurt escape my throat

Days like this make me wish praying worked for me
I would beg for my air back
Beg to feel like the child I never was
to let this life work out

Instead I let myself sob
I mean really sob
Noise and all until my throat gives out
until I can breathe enough to drive
Habitually telling myself
the low-income lullaby I learned
*No groceries this week*
*At least I have enough cash for the dollar menu*

But at home I drink some water
Take a breath
Do my work
Fix my hair and face
Grab a different card
Go back to the store
Pay for my groceries and think
This must be what healing is

## 30

Healing can look like tears sizzling in an egg pan
as touch-starved loneliness seasons my breakfast
Then resisting harmful habits by writing between bites

It can look like sobbing naked in the bathroom mirror
Then collapsing on the shower floor
and thinking to myself
At least I'm showering today

It can look like scraping at my nail polish
instead of my forearms
Then bruising my kneecaps
from crying my fears onto the living room floor
Then picking up my pen between breaths

Healing can look like laying in bed for 13 hours
clean and lonely
not wanting to tell anyone
because I am supposed to be okay
Then texting my best friend anyway
because she has seen all parts of me
and loves me whole
It looks like letting her love me through this
Then scrolling my camera roll
remembering people love me
even if they haven't talked to me in weeks

Healing can be painful in private
when all of my triggers converge
giving me another night of 8 p.m. bedtime
becoming 1 a.m. breakdown
until my eyes finally give out and I sleep for a little while

It can look like getting rid of old prescriptions
because the thought crossed my mind
one too many times
Then finally facing this poem
because my people deserve to know

However healing can also look like
the decade-old lily plant from Momma's funeral
finally flowering under my care
Then experimenting with fresh recipes for fun
and my body embracing the new flavors

It can look like my usual table
at my usual coffeeshop
writing my thoughts as the fresh grounds
cool enough to sip
Then building consistency and calm for myself
while holding my heart in a notebook

Healing can look like my left shoulder
showing more color than my right
because I've been driving my way
through a summer of loving myself
and the driver's seat always gets more of the sunlight

It can look like letting my legs feel vitamin D
for the first time in years
while listening to jazz in the sunset park
Then remembering how I feel myself in the music

It can look like hoping one day I'll be the older lady
who can't stay seated when everyone else is
because the sway can't stay in one place

Healing is planning a celebration
for my third decade
the one I never thought I'd see
and am now eager to ring in
Then recognizing that all of these thoughts mean
I finally want to grow old

## THE ALCHEMIST

I once gave up on a life of alchemy
a life of transforming my hurt into a golden lyric

Instead I followed a roster of expected goals
ones that led me to a career
writing of agronomy then annuities
Hiding my agony in secure paychecks and PTO trips

I found myself stagnant in a dead-end desert
Ignoring my instincts placed me in corporate purgatory
Until I was faced with the decision
Either stay put and play with wicked politics
or follow the ambiguous path of alchemy

I didn't make a choice in haste
I let the vapors of fear and sacrifice
fill my head for years
Kept myself sitting in the sand listening to the wind

But taking that time taught me of diligence and intention
It taught me that I never desired the expected

The lessons I learned there forced me
to notice the omens all around me
forced me to stop using logic as an excuse to stay stuck
forced me to hear the madcap energy
waiting past the desert

The lessons I learned there told me
that if I chose to heed my heart
I could become the glorious alchemist
I was always intended to be

And so I chose
to pick the path of pens and paycheck uncertainty

And I don't know how this story will end
But I know I'm finally following the life
I was always capable of

# ACKNOWLEDGEMENTS

"Behemoth" and "To The New Daughter of My Ex-Step Father" were originally published by Pile Press in *Issue 006* (May 2023).

"My Compass" was originally published by *Spirit Lake Review* (April 2023).

"To My Younger Brothers" was a finalist and originally published in the *2024 Central Avenue Poetry Prize* and is reprinted courtesy of Central Avenue Poetry."

The following poems were published in the *2023 Poetry Potluck* anthology (February 2024) by Kelsey Bigelow and Caleb "The Negro Artist" Rainey: "Look Closer," "Behemoth," "Silver Linings," "Allow Me to Reintroduce Myself," "I Wish I Didn't Relate to Their Exhaustion," "Welcome to My Concinnity," and "The Alchemist."

The following poems originally appeared as spoken word poems on Kelsey Bigelow's album, *Depression Holders and Secret Keepers* (September 2021): "Digression," "My Poems Now," "Poetic Trigger Warning," "Learned Instinct," "Atelophobia: The Fear of Imperfection," "Tree of Weeds," "Dysthymia: Persistent Depressive Disorder," "My Bed Called Me Again Today," "Poets are Born to Be Sad," "Reasons Don't Always Exist," "Autophobia: The Fear of Being Alone," "Asking for Help: An Open Letter," and "You are Not Inanimate Just Because You Have Depression"

# THANK YOU

Dad. For growing with me. For having the hard conversations and learning with me. For accepting me and seeing the value in the work I do. For the laughter and never-ending handshake. I'm honored to call you a friend. I love you so much.

Stephanie. For being the first person who ever validated my mental health. For seeing all parts of me and loving me whole. For being my constant for more than a decade and reading every poem I've ever written. I love you more than I'll ever be able to describe.

Caleb. For seeing me as The Alchemist I was always intended to be, even before I did. For consistently encouraging me and my growth. For listening to each version of this book that I envisioned. I am eternally grateful for your friendship and your existence.

Jen. For the guidance and gentleness you showed me as I put in the work to begin healing. For validating me, teaching me, and showing me just how right my instincts are. The growth shown in this collection has a lot to do with your commitment to me in each session.

Des Moines Poetry Workshop. For holding me to a higher standard. For the many rounds of revisions you kindly saw these poems through. For being a source of comfort and laughter at every writing night and critique group. I love our community, and this collection wouldn't exist without each of you.

# ABOUT THE POET

Kelsey Bigelow is a spoken word and page poet based in Des Moines. In her work, she molds incredibly specific emotions into something human, digestible, and cathartic. She is on a mission to show people two things: 1. You can live the life you dream, and 2. It does get better.

She is the author of *Far From Broken* (2024), *The Coffee Cherry* (2023), *Depression Holders and Secret Keepers* (2021), and *Sprig of Lilac* (2018). Her work is published in or forthcoming with *Central Avenue Publishing, Pile Press, Lyrical Iowa, Backchannels Journal, Spirit Lake Review*, and elsewhere. Kelsey is a 2024 Pushcart Prize nominee, a 2023 Button Poetry Video Contest Finalist, and a 2023 *Central Avenue Poetry Prize* shortlist finalist.

Kelsey is the founder and leader of the Des Moines Poetry Workshop, the chair for the Iowa Poetry Association Poetry Slam, the co-tournament director for the BlackBerry Peach National Poetry Slam, and more.

Get to know Kelsey at kelkaybpoetry.com

www.ingramcontent.com/pod-product-compliance
Ingram Content Group UK Ltd.
Pitfield, Milton Keynes, MK11 3LW, UK
UKHW041640190726
13854UKWH00006B/2603